Picture credits: Franklin Watts: p10; Getty Images: p18-19 (Gene Lincoln), p25 (Chuck Keeler); The Hutchison Library: p10 top (Robert Francis), p11 (Robert Francis), p15 (Robert Francis), p17 (Robert Francis), p26 bottom (Robert Francis); Image Bank: p5 and p11 (Romilly Lockyer) p8-9 (Michael Grecco), p14 (David de Lossy), p23 bottom (Dan Esgro), p26 top (Steve Krongard); Robert Harding: cover (Roger Evans), p6-7 (Tony Gervis), p16; Safeway: p23 top; The Stockmarket: p20, p27.

Editor: Kyla Barber
Art Director: Robert Walster
Designer: Diane Thistlethwaite
Illustrator: Teri Gower

First American edition 1998 by Franklin Watts
A Division of Grolier Publishing
Sherman Turnpike
Danbury, CT 06816

Visit Franklin Watts on the Internet at:
http://publishing.grolier.com

Library of Congress Cataloging-in-Publication Data

Pluckrose, Henry Arthur.
  In the Supermarket / Henry Pluckrose.
        p.   cm. —— (Machines at work)
  Includes index.
  Summary: Photographs and simple text present some of the different machines used in a large supermarket, including fork lifts, scales, pricing machines, and conveyor belts.
  ISBN 0-531-14498-4 (lib. bdg.)   0-531-15357-6 (pbk.)
  1. Excavating machinery——Juvenile literature. 2 Underground construction—— Juvenile literature. [1. Excavating machinery. 2. Underground construction. 3. Underground areas.] I. Title. II. Series: Pluckrose, Henry Arthur. Machines at work.
  TA732.P58   1999
  624.1 '52' 028——dc21

GROLIER
PUBLISHING

© 1998 Franklin Watts
96 Leonard Street
London
EC2A 4RH

Printed in Belgium

MACHINES AT WORK

In the Supermarket

Henry Pluckrose

W
FRANKLIN WATTS
A Division of Grolier Publishing
NEW YORK • LONDON • HONG KONG • SYDNEY
DANBURY, CONNECTICUT

A supermarket is a large store. It sells many different kinds of things.

Food and other goods are delivered to the supermarket in trucks. The truck is unloaded by a forklift.

forklift

The boxes of food
are carried on a
stock cart

a stock cart

and put out on the shelves.

A pricing machine
sticks the price on each item.

When a customer arrives
at the supermarket,
an electric eye
tells the doors to open.

electric eye

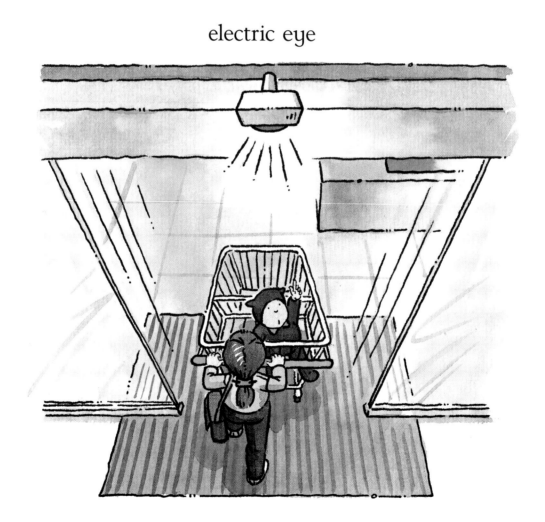

The customer takes
a shopping cart or a basket.
These are used to
carry the groceries.

Fresh fruits and vegetables
have to be weighed
to find out how much they cost.

A scale displays
the weight and price of the food.

scale

All supermarkets
sell bread and cakes.

Some may even
have a bakery.

At the delicatessen counter
there are all kinds
of cheeses and meats.
The meat is sliced by a machine.

Customers take a number
from the ticket machine
and wait their turn.

The employees must
make sure they have
clean hands when
they cut and wrap food.

Some foods are frozen and are kept in freezers. This keeps them from going bad.

Butter, milk, cream, and yogurt
are kept cool in refrigerators.
Electricity is used to power
the refrigerators and freezers.

In some places customers
are given scanners
before they shop.

scanner

The scanner machine
reads the bar code on each item
and adds up the cost
of the groceries.

The bar code contains
the price of the item.

41175 80073

23

The shopping cart
is pushed to the checkout.

The groceries are put on
a conveyor belt, which
carries them to the cash register.

Large supermarkets
have many checkouts.

Some cash registers
have a special scanner
to read the bar codes.

Another machine
adds up the prices
and prints out
a receipt.

The groceries are packed
into bags, and the
customer goes home
by car, bus, or bicycle.

Glossary

bar codes contain the price of an item.

cash registers add up the prices and then print out a receipt.

checkouts are where you pay for your groceries and pack them up.

conveyor belt is a moving surface..

refrigerator

electric eye

electric eyes tell the doors to open as you come near.

forklifts lift and move heavy items.

scanners read the bar codes on food and other items.

pricing machines stick bar codes or price labels onto food packages.

Index

scanner

checkout